C000263470

Keep this pocket-sized ....
you are visiting Lancaster, Morecambe and
Heysham.

Whether you are in your car or on foot, you will
enjoy an evocative journey back in time. Compare
the Lancaster, Morecambe and Heysham of old with
what you can see today—see how the streets and
buildings of the city of Lancaster have changed,
and how the holiday resort of Morecambe has
developed; look at fine details such as lamp-posts,
shop fascias and trade signs. See the many alterations
to the region that have taken place during our lives,
and which we may have taken for granted.

At the turn of a page you will gain fascinating
insights into the unique history of Lancaster,
Morecambe and Heysham.

FRANCIS FRITH'S
pocket ALBUM

LANCASTER, MORECAMBE AND HEYSHAM

A POCKET ALBUM

Adapted from an original book by
CLIFF HAYES

FRITH
BOOK Co

First published in the United Kingdom in 2003 by
Frith Book Company Ltd

ISBN 1-85937-731-9

Text and Design copyright © Frith Book Company Ltd
Photographs copyright © The Francis Frith Collection

The Frith photographs and the Frith logo are reproduced under licence from Heritage
Photographic Resources Ltd, the owners of the Frith archive and trademarks

All rights reserved. No photograph in this publication may be sold to a third party other
than in the original form of this publication, or framed for sale to a third party. No parts
of this publication may be reproduced, stored in a retrieval system, or transmitted, in any
form, or by any means, electronic, mechanical, photocopying, recording or otherwise,
without the prior permission of the publishers and copyright holder.

British Library Cataloguing in Publication Data

Lancaster, Morecambe and Heysham—A Pocket Album
Adapted from an original book by Cliff Hayes

Frith Book Company Ltd
Frith's Barn, Teffont,
Salisbury, Wiltshire SP3 5QP
Tel: +44 (0) 1722 716 376
Email: info@francisfrith.co.uk
www.francisfrith.co.uk

Printed and bound in Great Britain by MPG, Bodmin

Front Cover: Morecambe Central Beach c1950 / M94022
*The colour-tinting is for illustrative purposes only, and is not intended to be
historically accurate.*

Frontispiece: Lancaster, the Town Hall 1912 / 64215

AS WITH ANY HISTORICAL DATABASE THE FRITH ARCHIVE IS CONSTANTLY
BEING CORRECTED AND IMPROVED AND THE PUBLISHERS WOULD
WELCOME INFORMATION ON OMISSIONS OR INACCURACIES

CONTENTS

FRANCIS FRITH
VICTORIAN PIONEER

Francis Frith, founder of the world-famous photographic archive, was a complex and multi-talented man. A devout Quaker and a highly successful Victorian businessman, he was philosophic by nature and pioneering in outlook. By 1855 he had already established a wholesale grocery business in Liverpool, and sold it for the astonishing sum of £200,000, which is the equivalent today of over £15,000,000. Now in his thirties, and captivated by the new science of photography, Frith set out on a series of pioneering journeys up the Nile and to the Near East.

INTRIGUE AND EXPLORATION

He was the first photographer to venture beyond the sixth cataract of the Nile. Africa was still the mysterious 'Dark Continent', and Stanley and Livingstone's historic meeting was a decade into the future. The conditions for picture taking confound belief. He laboured for hours in his wicker dark-room in the sweltering heat of the desert, while the volatile chemicals fizzed dangerously in their trays. Back in London he exhibited his photographs and was 'rapturously cheered' by members of the Royal Society. His reputation as a photographer was made overnight.

VENTURE OF A LIFE-TIME

By the 1870s the railways had threaded their way across the country, and Bank Holidays and half-day Saturdays had been made obligatory by Act of Parliament. All of a sudden the working man and his family were able to enjoy days out, take holidays, and see a little more of the world.

With typical business acumen, Francis Frith foresaw that these new tourists would enjoy having souvenirs to commemorate their days out. For the next thirty years he travelled the country by train and by pony and trap, producing fine photographs of seaside resorts and beauty spots that were keenly bought by millions of Victorians. These prints were painstakingly pasted into family albums and pored over during the dark nights of winter, rekindling precious memories of summer excursions. Frith's studio was soon supplying retail shops all over the country, and by 1890 F Frith & Co had become the greatest specialist photographic publishing company in the world, with over 2,000 sales outlets, and pioneered the picture postcard.

FRANCIS FRITH'S LEGACY

Francis Frith had died in 1898 at his villa in Cannes, his great project still growing. The archive he created continued in business for another seventy years. By 1970 it contained over a third of a million pictures showing 7,000 British towns and villages.

Frith's legacy to us today is of immense significance and value, for the magnificent archive of evocative photographs he created provides a unique record of change in the cities, towns and villages throughout Britain over a century and more. Frith and his fellow studio photographers revisited locations many times down the years to update their views, compiling for us an enthralling and colourful pageant of British life and character.

We are fortunate that Frith was dedicated to recording the minutiae of everyday life. For it is this sheer wealth of visual data, the painstaking chronicle of changes in dress, transport, street layouts, buildings, housing, engineering and landscape that captivates us so much today, offering us a powerful link with the past and with the lives of our ancestors.

Computers have now made it possible for Frith's many thousands of images to be accessed almost instantly. The archive offers every one of us an opportunity to examine the places where we and our families have lived and worked down the years. Its images, depicting our shared past, are now bringing pleasure and enlightenment to millions around the world a century and more after his death.

LANCASTER, MORECAMBE AND HEYSHAM

AN INTRODUCTION

THE AREA we cover in this book is one of the most fascinating areas in the whole North of England. Lancaster, with its river position and antiquity, is the centre of our attention, but the areas at every compass point out of Lancaster have a history all of their own, and also a different face for the visitor both today and in the past. They include the ancient village of Heysham and its unique St Patrick's chapel on the headland; Overton, a village where time seems to pass slowly; and Sunderland Point, where the tide, not traffic lights, controls the main road. To the north, we have Halton, once the capital of the area, and Bolton-le-Sands, an ancient cross-roads. Head west, and we are in Morecambe; go east, and we are in the back roads and quietness of Quernmore, once an ancient forest and hall. Glasson Dock and its industrial environment lies to the south-west, along with the ancient and almost deserted area around Cockersands Abbey.

Once the castle and courts of Lancaster had been established, the city became the judicial centre for every court in the area; even the Leet and Baron courts for Overton and the Forest Court for Quernmore were held at Lancaster. The parliamentary area of Lancaster stretched down as far as Fulwood.

MORECAMBE

CENTRAL BEACH c1950 / M94022

THE CITY
OF
LANCASTER

THE ANCIENT city of Lancaster gave its name not only to the Palatine County, but also to a royal house. The Tudors were descendants of the House of Lancaster, and the Duke of Lancaster was part of the Tudor dynasty.

The name of Lancaster's river was originally the Lon, meaning health-giving. The Roman name for fort, 'castra', became 'ceaster' in Anglo-Saxon, so the fort on the Lon became Lonceaster, and then over time Lancaster.

LANCASTER

FROM SUNNY HILL c1885 / 18083

The old Town Hall was erected around 1781 on the site of an earlier town hall. Major Thomas Jarratt was the designer of the building, which opened in 1783. Market Square is the open area in front of the Town Hall, and Market Street runs to the left. The locals liked the large Tuscan portico and its four plain columns. The cupola and top were designed by Thomas Harrison, and were added just after the building opened. Harrison also designed Skerton Bridge. The total cost of the building was £2,054 13s 7d, including a £20 bonus that Mr Dickinson, one of the builders, had thought due to him.

LANCASTER

THE TOWN HALL 1886 / 18091

LANCASTER
CHURCH STREET 1886 / 18092

We are looking down the street, away from the parish church, which gave the street its name. Church Street was never as busy or popular as Market Street. In Church Street stands the building (now the Conservative Club) where Bonnie Prince Charlie stayed twice in 1745. The first time was in October 1745, when he was heading south, full of hope and ready to regain the throne of England; the second time was in December 1745, when he was in retreat and heading north.

Williamson Park was a gift from the Williamson family; it was begun by Joseph Williamson, and continued by his son (later Lord Ashton) in memory of his father. It was a magnificent gift, and is Lancaster's largest park. The Williamson family started making table baize, then known as American cloth, during the 1830s. They also made linoleum; they were at one time the largest manufacturer of this material, and exported it all over the world.

LANCASTER

THE PARK FOOTBRIDGE c1885 / 18098

The River Lune and the town of Lancaster are viewed from the New Bridge, or the Skerton Bridge as it is now called. The bridge in our photograph is the Greyhound Road Bridge; it replaced the very first bridge, the medieval Old Bridge, which led directly to Bridge Hill and China Lane, which was only 8ft wide. This is the spot where the Romans built their ford to cross the River Lune; today the new Century Footbridge is being built here.

LANCASTER

FROM THE BRIDGE 1891 / 28599

This is one of Lancaster's establishments which was allowed a Royal connection. Lancaster Royal Grammar School was founded in 1235, and in 1472 it was endowed by one John Gardyner. It moved to the site we see here on East Road in 1891, just before our photograph was taken.

LANCASTER

THE GRAMMAR SCHOOL 1891 / 28602

Here we see the Grammar School from another angle, looking from East Road back into the city. Being on the far side of the Lancaster Canal from the centre, the school was considered to be out in the country, and the air was good for the boys. The building is still there today; it is now a Grant Maintained school. The tower of St Peter's Roman Catholic Cathedral can be seen in the background.

LANCASTER

THE GRAMMAR SCHOOL 1896 / 37373

LANCASTER

THE CASTLE GATEWAY 1896 / 37368

Built in 1796-8 on the site of the original moat, the Shire Hall of Lancaster Castle is a fascinating building. It was built to do the business of the Shire; it contains over six hundred heraldic shields, and the coat of arms of every sovereign since Richard I. In the castle is a library, and in it is kept all the Laws of England since 1225. Court sittings permitting, we can tour the castle today and see much of this fascinating place, including the condemned cell, and an early gallows.

LANCASTER

THE CASTLE, SHIRE HALL 1896 / 37370

The Royal Lancaster Infirmary is pictured in the year this building was opened by the Duke and Duchess of Gloucester, later to be George V and Queen Mary. Lancaster's first dispensary opened in 1781, established by Dr Campbell; there had been a small dispensary and a convalescent house in Lancaster before this. When the foundation stone of this building was laid in 1849 it was the start of Lancaster's first proper hospital. It is still there today, but is now surrounded by a mass of modern hospital buildings.

LANCASTER

THE INFIRMARY 1896 / 37378

We are looking up Church Street towards St Mary's Parish Church and the Priory. The printing offices of the Lancaster Guardian was the second building on the right. Church Street was used as an open market on Lancaster Fair days. As the town was important, its Charter allowed four of these Fair Days—3 April, 1 May, 5 July and 10 October, which was also the Winter Fair and Hiring Day. Lancaster's first Charter of 1199 gave Wednesday and Saturday as market days.

LANCASTER

CHURCH STREET 1896 / 37381

We are in Market Square. The strange pole erected on the roof is the local telephone system. In the early years, all subscribers had their own separate line from the switchboard to their home or business. This led to a hundred or so separate wires heading over the roof-tops on poles and wooden constructions, as we see here. The Police Station and Fire Station, now the Library, are just on the right of the square. The corporation started making plans to move out of the old town hall as early as 1898, and bought a site in Dalton Square. It was over ten years later, in November 1910, that the staff moved out.

LANCASTER

THE TOWN HALL 1903 / 50057

Lancaster's large, ornate Queen Victoria Monument must be one of the finest in the country. When the old Queen died after more than sixty years on the throne, England threw itself into the building of a plethora of monuments, each one trying to be better and different. Given by Lord Ashton in 1907, this one has Queen Victoria in bronze guarded by four bronze lions, symbols of Great Britain. In the panels below are the great Victorians who flourished during the Queen's long reign, including Lord Derby, Robert Peel, Cobden, Bright, Thackeray, Tennyson, and Lancaster-born Richard Owen. The sculptor was Herbert Hampton.

LANCASTER

THE QUEEN VICTORIA MONUMENT 1912 / 64217

LANCASTER

THE TOWN HALL 1912 / 64218

This fine view shows Lancaster's new town hall, seen from Dalton Square. The Town Hall, another gift from Lord Ashton, had opened in 1909; it was designed by E W Mountford, who was the architect of the Old Bailey in London. The building incorporated the Central Police Station, so there were cells and a Police Court as well as a Civic Hall. The local furniture makers Waring and Gillow provided the furniture.

LANCASTER

THE TOWN HALL 1912 / 64215

Here we have a view of Dalton Square, the Town Hall, and the Queen Victoria monument. It was in Dalton Square that the cattle and livestock markets were held when Market Square had proved too small. Lancaster Council had always intended to move its town hall here, and had already purchased the land for this purpose about fifteen years before the new town hall opened.

Williamson Park was begun in the late 1860s as a scheme for the unemployed; they were to turn the bleak moorland and the quarries, that had once provided so much stone for the building of Lancaster, into a charming and interesting park. Work improving the park carried on for over twenty-five years. It was James Williamson, who had made his money in linoleum, who paid for the park, and his son (also James), later Lord Ashton, carried on the support. Here we see the lake and fountain, and the Ashton Memorial towering over the landscape.

LANCASTER

WILLIAMSON PARK 1912 / 64219

When his second wife Jessie died, Lord Ashton, son of James Williamson, decided to erect a monument to her. The Taj-Mahal of Lancaster, it rises 220ft to dominate the highest spot over the city; its green copper domed roof stands out for miles. Work started in 1907, and the monument was complete in 1909. The Memorial fell into disrepair in the 1970s; restoration work started in 1984, and the Memorial re-opened to the public on 22 May 1987.

LANCASTER

THE ASHTON MEMORIAL 1912 / 64220

Cable Street is one of the older streets of Lancaster, though not one of the medieval streets. China Street, St Leonard's Gate, Penny Street, Church Street and Market Street formed the original layout of the town from 1610, as we can see from Speed's map of Lancashire, which had an inset showing the county's capital, Lancaster. The area captured in our picture is known as Fleet Square; beside the photographer is Water Street, which led to the early crossing-place of the River Lune.

LANCASTER

THE CHURCH, FROM CABLE STREET 1912 / 64221

This view from Skerton Bridge looks back down the River Lune to Lancaster. The bridge we can see here is a railway bridge built by the 'Little North Western', who constructed a line to Morecambe in 1849; their station was at Green Ayre. Our view clearly shows the terraced housing, built on the north side of the Lune outside the old city walls, where Lune Terrace and Derby Road are today.

LANCASTER

THE RIVER LUNE, FROM SKERTON BRIDGE 1918 / 68328A

Lancaster developed on the east slopes of the castle and church. This area was once called Kirk Lancastre. All the buildings of early and medieval Lancaster were in the area in front of the castle gateway. This left the area behind the castle free for development, and open spaces and industrial buildings appeared in the mid Victorian period. Our photograph was taken from Giant Axe Field; the area behind the photographer, known as Marsh, had at the time been developed as a linoleum and oilskin manufacturing plant.

LANCASTER

THE CRICKET GROUND 1918 / 68330

A winged angel guards this tribute to the 'Honoured Memory of the Men of Lancaster Who Gave Their Lives in the Great War 1914-18'. This is not the only tribute to the fallen heroes; there is also a bronze statue by Jennie Delahunt of two soldiers sharing water, and round it there were cottages built for the returned heroes in a 'village' designed by Thomas Mawson.

LANCASTER

THE WAR MEMORIAL 1925 / 77913

31

We are looking over Lancaster and the outer parts of the castle from the higher inner ramparts. This large, square Norman keep with its 10ft-thick walls was restored on orders from Queen Elizabeth I. We can see the round tower added by King John, and the back of the famous John of Gaunt Gateway; the Ashton Memorial, looking like St Paul's in London, stands out from the murk of Lancaster behind. Part of the courtyard below was used to bury victims who were hung publicly outside the castle walls.

LANCASTER

THE VIEW FROM THE CASTLE 1927 / 80504

LANCASTER

A CASTLE WARDEN 1927 / 80507

The parish church of St Mary's was formerly the Priory. There has been a Roman basilica, a Saxon shrine and a Norman church on this site, long before the present church was built. The only Norman parts of today's church are the stones used in the re-building of the south doorway. There is also a small refuge room in the tower with a Saxon doorway and remnants from previous churches. Here we see the aisle to the left of the main church, which is the King's Own Memorial Chapel, a museum within a church. The white ensign flown by HMS 'Lancaster' hangs here among the flags flown at many famous battles.

LANCASTER

PARISH CHURCH, THE KING'S OWN MEMORIAL CHAPEL 1927 / 80527

LANCASTER

FROM CASTLE HILL c1950 / L10007

We are looking down Castle Hill, by the wall of Lancaster Castle. St Mary's Promenade is to the left, going up to the church. The Judge's Lodgings are at the bottom of Castle Hill down the lane. It would be up this walk that the Assize Judge and his entourage would walk on Assize Court days; the judge's man would carry the black cap used for passing the sentence of death.

LANCASTER

THE CASTLE c1950 / L10029

We are looking down from Castle Park to Castle
Hill and the city beyond. The Castle gateway is out
of shot on the left.

LANCASTER

FROM THE CASTLE c1950 / L10039

LANCASTER

MARKET STREET c1950 / L10042

We can see the old town hall with its apex roof peeping out on the left hand side, 100 yards up the street. Now a museum, it includes among its collection all the charters granted to Lancaster. The Tetley sign on the right of the street marks the John of Gaunt Hotel, which is still there today; it has plenty of character and eccentricity.

This is the very top of Market Street as we turn out of Castle Hill. The road coming in 100 yards down on the right is King Street, the A6 and the original road north; we can see that even fifty years ago it was one-way (note the no entry signs), showing that Lancaster had traffic problems even then. The Post Office and the King's Arms Hotel on the right are still there today.

LANCASTER

MARKET STREET C1950 / L10038

This is one of Lancaster's main shopping streets. Note the radio shop on the right—in country districts, the radio, with its BBC Home and Light programmes, helped people to keep in touch. Lancaster is on the edge of the Lake District, and an important point on routes both north and south. The National Cyclists Union and others would recommend a stop such as the 'Cyclists Rest' Bed & Breakfast, on the left above Babyland.

LANCASTER

PENNY STREET c1950 / L10044

SEASIDE
MORECAMBE

THE SEASIDE town of Morecambe, situated on Morecambe Bay, has wonderful views of the hills of the Lake District. The brine-tinged air from the bay, softened by the fresh air flowing in from across the Lake District, produced what Morecambe does best - a relaxing and exhilarating environment for a break or holiday. The whole area has been designated one of Outstanding Natural Beauty, and the Bay itself is one of Europe's best habitats for migrating birds.

Much maligned, Morecambe has always had to compete with other Lancashire seaside towns, and this does show in its history. The town started life as Poulton; then, to avoid confusion with another Poulton near Blackpool, it became Poulton-le-Sands—the other was Poulton-le-Fylde. Poulton-le-Sands is mentioned in the Domesday Book. The ancient fishing village of Bare was just to the north of Poulton, and was the home of the famous Morecambe Bay Shrimpers. Poulton-le-Sands, Bare and Torrisholme came together to form Morecambe around 1860, although the area had already started to develop as a seaside resort when the railway arrived in around 1849.

This early photograph shows the front at Morecambe over 110 years ago. Local fishermen used their boats to offer trips round the bay, which supplemented their income from catching shrimps and mussels. When the summer visitors arrived, some of the boats would be spruced up so as to turn to catching holiday-makers instead of fish.

MORECAMBE

THE ESPLANADE 1888 / 21076

MORECAMBE

THE CENTRAL PIER 1888 / 21080

There were two piers at Morecambe in the past. This one is the Central Pier, opened in 1869 to give visitors and holiday-makers a change—they could walk over the water and look down on the sea. When the pier first opened, there were no buildings or pavilions at the end. Holiday-makers staying the week could purchase a weekly ticket for only a shilling (5p), and stroll over the water for a full seven days.

'The sands', says the Frith title, but as you can see, central Morecambe has always had a pebble beach, especially at high tide. The stone jetty that we can see in the background was the main terminal for ships to Ireland and the Isle of Man, until Heysham Harbour was cut in the 1900s. The broad, stone-built jetty included sheds as shelter for passengers, as well as loading and unloading facilities, and trains could also back onto the pier, as we see in our photograph. Bathing machines are still in evidence at the edge of the water in this picture, and Morecambe was the proud possessor of about twenty of them when our photograph was taken. Locals always referred to them as 'vans'.

MORECAMBE

THE SANDS 1888 / 21078

In 1896, Morecambe opened a second pier, known as West End Pier, which is the one we see here in our picture. The building of a lavish pavilion at the end of this pier motivated the Central Pier to build a theatre at the end of their pier. The West End Pier was destroyed in a storm in November 1977; it was declared unsafe, and was demolished soon after.

MORECAMBE

WEST END PIER 1896 / 37387

The southern part, towards Heysham, soon developed as the more genteel side of the resort, with smart hotels; it was thought to be a little superior. The area today is known as Sandylands. Our horse tram is wending its way from Upper Heysham back to Morecambe. Today there is a very popular walk along the promenade between Morecambe and Heysham.

MORECAMBE

THE SOUTH END 1896 / 37386

This lovely view of the Promenade looks north towards Hest Bank, with the Central Pier in the background. Central Pier reacted in grand style to the opening of the West End Pier by building a pavilion at the end. It soon gained the nick-name 'the Taj Mahal', and indeed it did resemble that famous building. This Lancashire-style Indian Pavilion burnt out in a fire in 1933; it was rebuilt in 1935, but it was not as grand as the original.

MORECAMBE

THE CENTRAL PIER AND THE ESPLANADE 1899 / 42857

MORECAMBE

THE PROMENADE 1899 / 42860

The pier, the sea, bracing air and excursions to Heysham and the Lakes—that was what the holiday-makers wanted, and that was what Morecambe provided. Because of its closeness to the northern border, it always had a 'Scotch Week' when workers from Glasgow and the surrounding area would descend and 'let loose'. It was a sort of Wakes Week, Scottish style; it was always in mid-July.

This is a busy scene. Walking and strolling, and taking in the sea air, was what the late Victorian holiday-makers demanded. Resorts from Morecambe down the coast through New Brighton to Llandudno in Wales provided the wide walk-ways where holiday-makers could stroll and pass the time of day with family and friends away from the traffic. Note all the traffic in this picture is horse-drawn.

MORECAMBE

THE PROMENADE 1899 / 42855

At the turn of the 20th century, late Victorians enjoy a walk above the water on West End Pier. The spaces between the planks meant that you could see the water below, and this added to the excitement and danger of the early piers.

MORECAMBE

WEST END PIER 1899 / 42867

The southern part of Morecambe was always referred to as the West End. Here we see the exclusive part of Morecambe, and our view takes in Morecambe Tower. Our view shows what working-class people did for their week's holiday: they sat and relaxed and took in the sea air.

MORECAMBE

WEST END 1899 / 42862

Horses are very prominent in our photograph: one brave horse cab is going through the waves, and horses from the 'vans' (bathing machines) are coming ashore. There would have been about one thousand people in Morecambe whose employment was looking after or working with the horses of the town at this time.

MORECAMBE

WEST END PROMENADE 1899 / 42864

Our late Victorian visitors were presented with a pebbly beach. We can see the stone jetty in the distance: it was still the main anchorage for ships when our photograph was taken. The just-paddling brigade stayed south of the Stone Pier, which was still a busy working port. It would continue to be so until Heysham opened in around 1904. The jetty was later rented to T W Wards, a ship breakers, and became quite a visitor attraction, with ships moored waiting to be broken up. In the years after the First World War, nearly half a million people paid to tour the ships waiting for the breakers' torch.

MORECAMBE

THE SANDS 1899 / 42870

MORECAMBE

WEST END PROMENADE 1903 / 50061

Here we see the area at the start of the West End Pier. By the early years of the 20th century, Morecambe had most of its major tourist attractions in place, things that would bring in the visitors for many years. The two piers were completed, and so was the promenade, complete with free shelters; there was a fun fair, and in 1890 Morecambe started an annual Music Festival, which proved very popular.

This is the area which was at the entrance to Central Pier; at this time it was the centre for visitors in Morecambe. This is reflected by the number of dining rooms we can see on our photograph. As well as the Star Dining Rooms and the Pier Head Dining Room on its left, we have another on the very right of our view. The Queen's Hotel is just to the right of the clock tower; it was one of the resort's main hotels at this time. If we look closely, we can see the tower still peeping over the rooftops on the left.

MORECAMBE

CENTRAL PROMENADE 1906 / 56104

The pavilion seen in our photograph was built in 1897 to dwarf the West End Pier dome that had just been completed. Locals soon found a nick-name for our end-of-the-pier Victorian edifice. They called it 'the Taj Mahal of Morecambe', and it was a wonderfully eccentric and ornamental building until it was burnt down in 1933.

MORECAMBE

CENTRAL PIER 1906 / 56106

The buildings beneath the tower were completed at the turn of the 20th century. Just like Blackpool today, our tower building contained a theatre (later a cinema), a ballroom and gardens. When the tower itself came down in about 1912, the tower building continued to be a centre for entertainment. About this time it was renamed the Gaumont and became a cinema, but it closed in 1959. It then became a ten pin bowling alley through the 'swinging sixties', and then a bingo hall.

MORECAMBE

THE TOWER BUILDING FROM CENTRAL PROMENADE c1950 / M94008

Our clock tower is showing signs of age in this photograph from
half a century ago. The marked two colours of brick are not so
easy to distinguish fifty years on from our earlier photographs.
The ornate clock tower was a gift to the town in 1905 from
Alderman J R Birkett.

MORECAMBE

THE CLOCK TOWER c1950 / M94014

MORECAMBE

CENTRAL PROMENADE c1950 / M94023

This view shows a mixed bag of transport. The horse carriages, which were a popular tourist taxi, are present at the head of Central Pier, while the post-war growth in the car industry is reflected in new and pre-Second World War cars. The large building on the left is Morecambe Winter Gardens, opened in 1878 as 'the People's Palace of Varieties & Aquarium'.

We are looking at the area that was between West End and Central Piers just before they both fell foul of the weather. The fair had grown and developed, and the council had opened Happy Mount Park (in 1927) to give holiday makers an even more memorable holiday. The Clarendon, on the right, was an old-established hotel.

MORECAMBE
WEST END PROMENADE c1950 / M94019

MORECAMBE

Jugs of tea are advertised on the left, and 'Walkie Photos' on the right. It is a pity that more effort was not put into saving one of Morecambe's piers in the late 1970s when they were still there; but those years were not a time when conservation or heritage featured much on the agenda. The Super Swimming Stadium had opened in 1936; as a promotion for the pool, a Miss Great Britain competition was started in Morecambe in 1945. In 1964 Marineland, Europe's first Oceanarium, opened on the old stone jetty.

Here we see the centre of Torrisholme, a quiet Morecambe suburb, on a
pleasant, sunny day. It is an old settlement—Domesday Book recorded
Torrisholme as Toredholme, and later still as Toroldesbi. The George
Hotel is on the right, next to Shaw's shop. In 1965 Torrisholme was
developing as a place to live for people working in Morecambe or
Lancaster; from here they could easily commute to work.

TORRISHOLME

THE SHOPPING CENTRE c1965 / T238014

This 'Happy Days' wagonette or country-style horse bus, harking back to transport in earlier days, is taking a party on a jaunt on a sunny day. Our photographer was lucky to catch the party who pose happily for him. They are probably regulars from the hotel, and are going on a specially-organised day out. Torrisholme was once a hamlet two miles north-west of Lancaster, and was one of the three villages which combined with Bare and Poulton-le-Sands to make up Morecambe around 130 years ago.

TORRISHOLME

A WAGONETTE AT THE GEORGE HOTEL c1965 / T238026

THE
VILLAGE
OF HEYSHAM

HEYSHAM IS a very ancient village, that can easily trace its history over 2,000 years. At one time there were two separate communities, Heysham Village, lower down, and higher Heysham around Heysham Hall, now an hotel. The fact that the village name is first recorded in the Domesday Book as Hessam leads historians to believe that the name comes from an early low German personal name, 'Hess'. The 'y' element did not come into the name until the middle 1600s. The spelling of the village name has changed a few times since it was first written: Heseym (1094), Hescam (1222) and Hesame (1463) are some of the variations. The other Heysham is the new harbour, opened at the very start of the 20th century in about 1903; there was also the famous Heysham Holiday Camp next to the harbour, known in the 1960s as Middleton Towers.

Heysham Parish Authorities came under the barony of Lancaster and the Poor Law Union of Caton. They ran the area until they were succeeded by the Heysham Urban District Council in 1899. The UDC amalgamated with Morecambe in 1928.

This charming view of the village of Heysham was taken from the cliff walk leading to Sandylands and Morecambe. At the time, tourism would support the village in the summer, and fishing in the winter months. We can see that the footpath is a well-worn one, so it must have been popular with visitors. The cliffs at Heysham are the first coming north after the Great and Little Orme at Llandudno; they presented the Victorian visitor with breathtaking views over to the Lake District.

HEYSHAM

THE VILLAGE 1895 / 35868

The origins of the parish church of St Peter on Heysham Head are lost in the mists of time. The earliest recorded date is 1080, when it was noted as an old Saxon church. There was probably an earlier church on this site, built by the Angles. Quite a bit of the Saxon stonework remains today, even though the church has been added to and enlarged. The original part is at the centre. Note the lack of standing gravestones in the graveyard around the church.

HEYSHAM

ST PETER'S CHURCH 1888 / 21072

We are looking at the leeward side from the entrance to the church-yard. Note how many standing headstones there are now, only four years after picture 21072. We can clearly see the 1864 extension, the lower part to the right with its own small entrance. This end of the church is in three parts, as we can tell by the three apex roofs. Today, when we visit this area around the altar and choir, we will find a wonderful small intimate part of the church cut off from the chancel by an oak screen, believed to have come from Cockersands Abbey.

HEYSHAM

ST PETER'S CHURCH 1892 / 30443

St Patrick himself is said to have been shipwrecked on the head; years later, monks came from his monastic foundation in Ireland and built this chapel in his memory. It dates from Saxon times, the 8th century, and one of the reasons it had stood so long in such an exposed spot is the mortar. It is ground-up sea shells, heated and mixed with boiling water to give a cement-like substance. It is the only example left in England of a single-cell Saxon chapel. Our Victorian ladies posing by the chapel add charm to our photograph—which apart from them could have been taken today.

HEYSHAM

ST PATRICK'S CHAPEL RUINS, HEYSHAM HEAD 1888 / 21071

These unique and mysterious stone coffins (ossuaries) are near St Patrick's chapel. Anything we say about these resting places cut into the rock is purely speculation. There are six here, and two more over by the chapel door. Carbon tests on the bones found in the coffins date from the 900s, yet the coffins are much, much earlier. The fence round the chapel and the barbed wire round the coffins is very surprising. Today, there are no fences up on the head—not even one to keep one away from the edge.

HEYSHAM

STONE COFFINS 1912 / 64229

This stone, which marked the grave of a Viking warrior, was his resting spot for over 1,000 years: it is from the 10th century. He had converted to Christianity; but though one side of the stone is carved with Christian symbols, the other side represents the pagan Viking heaven. In 1961 it was taken inside the church for protection against the weather and against too many visitors running their hands over the stone. Though there are other hogback stones, this is the finest and best preserved.

HEYSHAM

THE PARISH CHURCHYARD, THE HOGBACK STONE 1912 / 64232

The rocky coast around Heysham Head provided excitement and danger for its Victorian and Edwardian visitors. No holiday in Morecambe or Lancaster was complete without a day at Heysham. Nicknames or folk names gave places added attraction to those day-trippers; here we see the rock formation known for many years as 'The Fairy Chapel'. Our two visitors seem impressed enough to pose for their photograph.

HEYSHAM

FAIRY CHAPEL ROCKS 1912 / 64233

HEYSHAM

THE FORESHORE c1947 / H81003

Post-war visitors gather and take in the fresh sea air on the rocky shore. The car is making its mark on leisure time, and petrol was available again after the war-time restrictions. Even then, parking in the village was a problem; these visitors have chosen to chance leaving their cars, motorbikes and motor-bikes with sidecars on the rocky beach.

We are at the top of Main Street, looking back down through the village from the bus station. Traffic will always be a problem to the small fishing village, and here we see the two old buildings which make the Main Street entrance narrow and restrict traffic. Coaches, omnibuses and so on have always had to park at the top of the street and let the visitors wander down. The large square building on the right had for many years a large brass weighing machine outside. For 6d the showman would 'Guess Your Weight'. You got your money back if he was not within 2-3lbs of your real weight when he weighed you straight afterwards.

HEYSHAM

THE VILLAGE 1947 / H81006

This charming view looks up Main Street from the shore. The wooden posts erected to mark out the gardens of the row stopped visitors peering through the windows, and helped give the inhabitants a little bit of privacy. A photographer waits to snap visitors; I wonder if he developed the prints in an hour—the slogan used to be 'pick up before you leave'. The Royal Hotel on the right, half-way up Main Street, is still there; like the village, it seems to have resisted change and modernisation. It is still today a lovely mish-mash of small rooms and cosy bars, and was still serving mild beer very recently.

HEYSHAM

MAIN STREET 1947 / H81005

HEYSHAM

COSY CORNER c1900 / H81301

The shore line at Heysham is owned by Queen Elizabeth II. The concrete sea defence to Morecambe has been constructed, and provides a sort of primitive promenade. Can you make out the concrete terraces that have been constructed on each side of the village slipway? As the tide is in, they are full of visitors in our photograph; the pebble beach is covered, so we see only the sandy bit of Heysham.

HEYSHAM

THE FORESHORE c1950 / H81002A

Heysham Tower was built by T J Knowles in about 1837, and it was the home of the Cawthra family. There was a lodge down in the village, and the estate of about 14 acres was laid out with attractive gardens and woods. When construction started on Heysham Harbour, the family moved out; it was bought by the Midland Railway, who were building the harbour. At the time of our photograph it was an hotel. In 1925 it became the Morecambe Bay Holiday Camp, with 400 campers in this building and another 100 men in permanent tents in the grounds. It later became Middleton Towers Holiday Camp.

HEYSHAM

HEYSHAM TOWER 1915 / H81014

HEYSHAM

THE DOCKS c1915 / H81009

It is a busy beach in the Swinging Sixties: these people are not day trippers to Heysham, but guests of Middleton Towers who have made their way to the beach for a day of free activity and entertainment. The holiday complex and Tower buildings are still standing.

HEYSHAM

HALF MOON BAY C1965 / H81027

DOUGLAS

VICTORIA PIER 1907 / 59160

In the years just after it opened, almost half of the passenger traffic from Heysham Harbour went to Douglas, Isle of Man. Heysham was a popular port with Yorkshire people, who found it easier to get to than Liverpool, Fleetwood and Holyhead, even further away. Here we see a mixed collection of vessels, including one of the Midland Railway ships.

Heysham became the centre for travel to the Isle of Man, and in 1923 the Fleetwood services were transferred there. 'Scotch Week' saw passenger numbers double, and Yorkshire Wakes Weeks kept the port busy. At this time the Isle of Man was a superior holiday venue, definitely something to mention in your circle of friends. If you went there, it meant that you had crossed the water, taken a little more effort, and almost gone abroad for your holiday. Here we see the Midland Railway ship 'Antrim' in Douglas Harbour, waiting to return to Heysham.

DOUGLAS

FROM DOUGLAS HEAD

1907 / 59152

GLASSON DOCK
AND THE
LANCASTER CANAL

IN 1780 the River Lune was silting up. The dock that had been established at Sunderland Point by Robert Lawson was having problems getting goods into and out of Lancaster, governed as it was by a tidal highway. Lancaster's solution was to build a dock near the village of Glasson.

Work began in 1783, and by 1790 the quays were in use; a year later, it was a fully operational port. Though it solved Lancaster's problems of import and export, it did nothing to improve her communications with the growing industrial heart of Lancashire to the south. The Lancaster Canal Company was formed in 1787, but it was 1819 before the canal to Preston opened. In 1826 the branch to Glasson Dock was completed, and the river and dock were connected to the canal system and Lancaster. The Glasson Dock branch, just three and a half miles with six locks, was the most important section of the Lancaster Canal as far as most Lancaster merchants were concerned.

This view shows the main dock, with the River Lune beyond. Our photographer is standing on the bridge over the lock which separates the dock from the Lancaster Canal basin. At the time of our photograph, ship repairing was still going on at Glasson, and the graving or dry dock was still in use. We see behind the dock a busy little port, though it was mostly used by coasters and Irish cargo boats.

GLASSON

THE DOCKS c1955 / G260003

GLASSON

THE DOCK c1950 / G260004

This is the main dock which gave its name to Glasson Dock, with a sailing ship tied up. The name Glasson is one of those names that historians dislike, because there is no known explanation for it. Old Norse has 'glas' meaning a river, so it could be 'the place on the river'—but that would be written 'Glason'. The first recorded mention of this tiny fishing community set on Fishnet Point was in 1587, and that was as Glasson.

After the turn of the 19th century, Glasson Dock was used more and more by pleasure craft. Wealthy mill owners and industrialists found it handy to leave their boats in the shelter of the dock or the canal basin, and leisure became more and more a source of income for Glasson Dock. Here we see only two working ships to four pleasure cruisers, though ships could only come and go into the dock on a rising or high tide. Our hotel has had a big facelift: it stands out white and ornate in Victoria Terrace, which contains a pub at either end.

GLASSON

THE DOCKS c1955 / G260026

GLASSON

We can take a closer look at that terrace. On the right you can see the Nissen huts put up in the 1939-45 war for soldiers and the Home Guard, who were based here to keep supplies flowing during the war years. This area is now the main car park for visitors. One of the gondolas from the big wheel at Blackpool ended its life as a cafe here, and stood just to the right of our picture.

We are actually inside the port area here; again we see the mixture of coasters, fishing vessels, yachts and pleasure craft. Even today the dock is like a living open-air museum, with old bits of machinery and rusting equipment around. Though the railway here closed in 1964 along with Condor Green Station, there are still lines and the odd wagon in the dock. The area around Glasson is teaming with wildlife, and is a bird watcher's paradise from Conder Green down to Cockerham Sands in the south. Swans and ducks live in the canal basin.

GLASSON

THE QUAY c1955 / G260012

Glasson Dock Bridge connects the two halves of the village. Because of its weight restrictions, many of the lorries going in and out of the dock had to go half a mile or more inland before a strong enough bridge could take them over to the West Quay. The bridge today has been rebuilt and strengthened to take the heavy traffic, and is fitted with traffic lights. West Quay was always the visitors' favourite, with its ice cream shop, cafe, fresh fish shop and the Dalton Arms.

GLASSON

THE BRIDGE c1965 / G260049

AROUND
LANCASTER

PEOPLE DASH north and head for the Lake District. Coaches convey thousands of day trippers east to visit the Yorkshire Dales. Both miss what is one of the loveliest and quietest areas of the North of England. It is almost like a huge secret, known only to walkers, nature lovers and those who live there. The Lune Valley to the north-east of Lancaster is truly one of the most unspoilt areas in the north; Pilling Moss lies to the south, Quernmore to the south-east and Overton Moss to the west, and all these areas surround the city with peaceful tranquillity. The great artist Turner appreciated this area, and many of his best paintings are of this part of the country. Ruskin appreciated the countryside surrounding Lancaster, and wrote lovingly of the old villages.

Maybe I should not tell the secret, but keep it, so that the area does not have the problems that the Lake District now faces. Too late —I have told you now. So do go and see for yourself, and then keep the secret from anyone else.

The village of Bolton-le-Sands sits astride the A6, four miles north of Lancaster. Our photograph shows both the village churches: the Roman Catholic spire is to the left and the Anglican tower to the right. In the Domesday Book the village was mentioned as 'Bodetone', meaning 'the dwelling house of Botl'. It was 1706 before the name became what it is today, a common old England name. The Parish of Bolton-le-Sands is 5,895 acres in size.

BOLTON-LE-SANDS

GENERAL VIEW 1898 / 41055

Here we have the old centre of the village, now by-passed by the main road. The Roman Catholic church of St Mary of the Angels with its free-standing spire dominates the centre of our photograph. Catholics started meeting in a barn in 1868, and this church was consecrated in 1884. The hotel on the left is the Blue Anchor Hotel; the name reminds us how near the sea is, only half a mile behind Wild Duck Farm. There has been an inn on this spot since 1706.

BOLTON-LE-SANDS

THE CATHOLIC CHURCH 1898 / 41059

This photograph shows the old village centre, looking from the Roman Catholic church of St Mary of the Angels. Carnforth Co-operative Society looked after the villagers' grocery needs. The building on the left with the pillars on each side of the door is the Blue Anchor Hotel, and Hall's Sweet Shop and Post Office stands between. Peeping out above the inn is the tower of St Michael's Church, one of the oldest in the district.

BOLTON-LE-SANDS

THE VILLAGE c1960 / B137022

This peaceful view shows the Lancaster Canal as it passes through Bolton-le-Sands. The canal arrived here in 1797, and transformed the village into a town. Between 1820 and 1849, passenger boats on the canal were the main form of transport between Kendal and Preston, and the Packet Boat Hotel, seen here, was one of the inns built for passengers so that they could eat on their journey or wait for the next boat.

BOLTON-LE-SANDS

THE CANAL c1960 / B137030

This is the road down to the shore (and Red Bank Farm). Red Bank is one of the spots from which you can cross the sands over to Kents Bank. In Victorian times, Bolton was a favourite spot for those who wanted a quiet peaceful holiday, and it became a welcome means of making money for the locals to take in visitors. Horse-drawn coaches and wagonettes would come from Morecambe and Lancaster, and local children would meet the visitors and sell them snacks and bunches of flowers.

BOLTON-LE-SANDS

SHORE ROAD c1965 / B137034

Brookhouse is an ancient village north-east of Lancaster just above Caton. It is at a junction on the old Caton to Claughton road, which we can see going off to the left. The inn on the right is the Black Bull, and Leslie Speckling was landlord at the time. The five hundred-year-old parish church tower of St Paul's shows up at the top of our photograph.

BROOKHOUSE

THE VILLAGE c1955 / B872003

BROOKHOUSE

THE VILLAGE c1955 / B872058

Our caption says Caton, which is correct, but only just: the wall to the left is the bridge over Tern Brook, and the houses we see are actually in Brookhouse. In front of the ancient oak are a set of steps known locally as the Fish Stones. History tells us that they were built as a counter and shop; here the monks from Cockersands Abbey brought salmon and other fish they had caught in the River Lune to sell to the villagers. Only monks were allowed to catch salmon, and the money they raised paid for their needs and candles.

CATON

THE DRUIDS' OAK C1955 / C473013

Carnforth, six miles north of Lancaster, has a place in history as a railway town. The Furness & Midland Railway and the London & North Western Railway opened a station at Carnforth between them in 1880, and it was always an important junction. Wolstencroft the chemist boasts that they serve General Drugs and Patent Medicines, Horse & Cattle Medicines and Thorleys Cattle Spice, as well as being Oil & Colour Merchants. They were also agents for the Caledonian Fire & Life Insurance and Ocean, Railway & General Accident. They sold sleeping powders, cures for influenza and butter colour. As well as all that, they even advertised 'Teeth Carefully Extracted'—this is reassuringly etched into the glass door.

CARNFORTH
MARKET STREET 1898 / 41032

Cockerham, the village, and Cockersands, the Abbey, both take their names from the River Cocker, which runs between them. Cockerham today is not actually on the river, which runs across the large Cockerham Moss. In the Domesday Book it is written as 'Cocreham'. The original village was burnt down in the 1600s and had to be completely rebuilt. The villagers left the burnt-out village and moved on to the main road, around the Manor Inn, seen here in our photograph.

COCKERHAM

THE VILLAGE c1955 / C599010

At the time of the Domesday Book, Halton was the main administrator of the area, and Lancaster was 'under' Halton, which lies three miles north-east of Lancaster. The River Lune runs south of the village, which has Saxon and Roman remains under today's sprawling housing estates. In the Domesday Book it was spelt as it is today; the name comes from either 'halgh', an ancient word for hill, or from an Icelandic invader named Hella who settled here.

HALTON

FROM THE RIVER C1955 / H506010

The River Lune has never suffered the amount of industrial pollution that its southern Lancashire sisters the Mersey and the Ribble have had. Here we see youngsters enjoying swimming and paddling in the river. The two bridges that cross the river here can be clearly seen in the background. Castle Hill is the highest spot in Halton, and this hill, above the church, is the place where Roman, Saxon, Danish and Norman defences have once stood.

HALTON

THE RIVER BANK AND THE BRIDGES c1960 / H506055

Hest was part of Bolton-le-Sands, and was a hamlet near Morecambe Bay. Hest Bank was the seaward side of the village, right at the southern side of the mouth of the River Kent. At one time, the area was referred to as Slyne with Hest. The Lancaster Canal Act was passed in 1792; the canal from Kendal to Carnforth opened first in 1797, and then this section opened, Bolton-le-Sands via Hest Bank to Lancaster. As soon as the canal opened, it proved an easier and more comfortable way of travelling and moving goods than along the poor roads that existed at the time.

HEST BANK

THE CANAL c1955 / H453003

Station Road led down to the railway station, now long gone. They called the main railway line from Crewe to Glasgow the West Coast Main Line, but here at Hest Bank is the only spot where you can actually see the coast and the sea beyond. Hest Bank is the name used for the whole settlement. Three forms of transport have cut through the area at various times: the main Roman road, later the A6, the Lancaster Canal, and the railways, all bringing prosperity and extra work to the area. The railway was so busy a century ago that a footbridge was built so that visitors did not have to wait to cross the line to get to the beach. We can see this bridge in our picture at the bottom of the road.

HEST BANK

STATION ROAD c1955 / H453001

HEST BANK

THE CENTRE c1960 / H453016

This is the A6 cross-roads, with 'Halt' signs painted on the road and squared T-shaped traffic signs gently controlling what little traffic there was. There are no yellow lines, no posts everywhere with instructions and restrictions—oh, it was such a gentle time for motor travel. The name Hest comes from 'hyrst' (a copse or wood), and the name was first recorded in 1184.

'A picturebook castle' is how the castle at Hornby has been described. Painted by the artist Turner, it became famous and was much visited. It was built by the Norman Montbegon family just after they arrived in Lancashire. They lived in the motte and bailey Castle Stede nearby while it was being constructed. Later it was owned by the Harrington family, who lost both father and son and heir in a Civil War battle. It is still a private residence today.

HORNBY

THE CASTLE c1910 / H454020

This picture of peace and tranquillity, though it was taken in 1918, could really have been taken in 1998 or even yesterday. Note the boathouse on the far bank. I wonder if these people were charged every time they used the canal, or if they paid a one-off or annual fee. In March 1895, the canal drained overnight owing to subsidence, and washed away the surface of Station Road, Hest Bank. Note the white paint on the bridge archway to make it stand out on dark winter mornings or in twilight.

LANCASTER
THE CANAL 1918 / 68332

The parish of Overton lies five miles south-west of Lancaster on the road to Sunderland Point. Tucked away in a very secluded corner below Heysham, this little village was mentioned in the Domesday Book as Ovretun; the name turns up very frequently in old documents, usually mentioning the church or a curate. The lovely old church here still retains its original Norman doorway. Overton means 'dwellings by (next to) the water', and the village used to flood at every high spring or autumn tide.

OVERTON

THE POST OFFICE c1960 / O121008

Over Kellet is a village off the main road, on the Arkholme road out of Bolton-le-Sands. Here we see the two monuments in the village centre. The nearest is the old village cross, and the new white pillar beyond it, with the high railing round it, was at this time the newly-erected memorial to those who never returned from the Great War in 1914-18. Later the old cross was turned into a memorial for the Second World War.

OVER KELLET

THE VILLAGE 1923 / 74161

The village of Quernmore is three miles south-east of Lancaster. Quernmore Park Hall lies just over a mile north of the village. A quern was a Roman hand-mill, and the moor behind the village had the ideal material to make these small mill-stones. Kvernberg is Old Norse for a mill-stone quarry. The village took its name from the great Quernmore forest which once covered this area. This photograph shows the cross-roads, where the motorist could get some refreshment and petrol in those days of more leisurely travel. The road behind us climbs up to Hare Appletree Fell.

QUERNMORE

THE CROSSROADS c1955 / Q17503

As we head north, Warton Crag is the first sign of the Lake District with its ancient limestone rocks. Behind Warton Crag, the Lake District really builds up its thrusting and stark peaks, softened over time with the water catchments that led to the lovely lakes. The village of Warton, shown here, lies sheltered beneath the Crag and looks peaceful, but it was a hard-working place to live in a century ago. Copper mining was one of the local industries, though farming was the main source of employment.

WARTON

THE CRAG 1898 / 41041

INDEX

PLEASE HELP US BRING FRITH'S PHOTOGRAPHS TO LIFE

Our authors do their best to recount the history of the places they write about. They give insights into how particular towns and villages developed, they describe the architecture of streets and buildings, and they discuss the lives of famous people who lived there. But however knowledgeable our authors are, the story they tell is necessarily incomplete.

Frith's photographs are so much more than plain historical documents. They are living proofs of the flow of human life down the generations. They show real people at real moments in history; and each of those people is the son or daughter of someone, the brother or sister, aunt or uncle, grandfather or grandmother of someone else. All of them lived, worked and played in the streets depicted in Frith's photographs.

We would be grateful if you would tell us about the many places shown in our photographs—the streets with their buildings, shops, businesses and industries. Describe your own memories of life in those streets: what it was like growing up there, who ran the local shop and what shopping was like years ago; if your workplace is shown tell us about your working day and what the building is used for now. With your help more and more Frith photographs can be brought to life, and vital memories preserved for posterity.

We will gradually add your comments and stories to the archive for the benefit of historians of the future. Wherever possible, we will try to include some of your comments in future editions of our books. Moreover, if you spot errors in dates, titles or other facts, please let us know, because our archive records are not always completely accurate—they rely on 150 years of human endeavour and hand-compiled records.

So please write, fax or email us with your stories and memories. Thank you!

CHOOSE ANY PHOTOGRAPH FROM THIS BOOK

for your FREE Mounted Print. Order further prints at half price

Fill in and cut out the voucher on the next page and return it with your remittance for £2.50 for postage, packing and handling to UK addresses (US $5.00 for USA and Canada). For all other overseas addresses include £5.00 post and handling. Choose any photograph included in this book. Make sure you quote its unique reference number eg. 42365 (it is mentioned after the photograph date. 1890 / 42365). Your SEPIA print will be approx 12" x 8" and mounted in a cream mount with a burgundy rule line (overall size 14" x 11").

Mounted Print
Overall size 14 x 11 inches

Order additional Mounted Prints at HALF PRICE - If you would like to order more Frith prints from this book, possibly as gifts for friends and family, you can buy them at half price (with no extra postage and handling costs) - only £7.49 each (UK orders), US $14.99 each (USA and Canada).

---

* IMPORTANT!

These special prices are only available if you order at the same time as you order your free mounted print. You must use the ORIGINAL VOUCHER on the facing page (no copies permitted). We can only despatch to one address.

Have your Mounted Prints framed (UK orders only) - For an extra £14.95 per print you can have your mounted print(s) framed in an elegant polished wood and gilt moulding, overall size 16" x 13" (no additional postage).

FRITH PRODUCTS AND SERVICES

All Frith photographs are available for you to buy as framed or mounted prints. From time to time, other illustrated items such as Address Books, Calendars, Table Mats are also available. Already, almost 50,000 Frith archive photographs can be viewed and purchased on the internet through the Frith website.

For more detailed information on Frith companies and products, visit

www.francisfrith.co.uk

For further information, trade, or author enquiries, contact:

The Francis Frith Collection, Frith's Barn, Teffont, Salisbury SP3 5QP

Tel: +44 (0) 1722 716 376 Fax: +44 (0) 1722 716 881 Email: sales@francisfrith.co.uk

Send completed Voucher form to:

UK and rest of world - The Francis Frith Collection, Frith's Barn, Teffont, Salisbury, Wiltshire SP3 5QP England

USA and Canada orders - Frith USA Inc, 11447 Canterberry Lane, Parker, Colorado, 80138 USA

If you need more space, please write your address on a separate sheet of paper.

Voucher for FREE and Reduced Price Frith Prints

Do not photocopy this voucher. Only the original is valid, so please fill it in, cut it out and return it to us with your order.

	Picture ref no	Page number	Qty	Mounted @ £7.49 UK @$14.99 US	Framed + £14.95 (UK only)	US orders Total $	UK orders Total £
1			1	Free of charge*	£	$	£
2				£7.49 ($14.99)	£	$	£
3				£7.49 ($14.99)	£	$	£
4				£7.49 ($14.99)	£	$	£
5				£7.49 ($14.99)	£	$	£
				£7.49 ($14.99)	£	$	£

Please allow 28 days for delivery

	* Post & handling	$5.00	£2.50
	Total Order Cost	US $	£

Title of this book ....

I enclose a cheque / postal order (UK) for £ .... $ ....
payable to 'Francis Frith Collection' (USA orders 'Frith USA Inc')

OR debit my Mastercard / Visa / Switch (UK) / Amex card / Discover (USA)
(credit cards only on non UK and US orders), card details below

Card Number

Issue No (Switch only)   Valid from (Amex/Switch)

Expires   Signature

Name Mr/Mrs/Ms ....

Address ....

....

....

Postcode/Zip.......................... Country ....

Daytime Tel No ....   Valid to 31/12/06

PAYMENT CURRENCY: We only accept payment in £ Sterling or US $.
If you are ordering **from any other country, please pay by credit card**, and you will be charged in one of these currencies.